20 Answers

~

Salvation

Jimmy Akin

Catholic
Answers
Press

20 Answers: Salvation

Jimmy Akin

© 2015 Catholic Answers

Published by Catholic Answers, Inc.
2020 Gillespie Way
El Cajon, California 92020
1-888-291-8000 orders
619-387-0042 fax
catholic.com

Printed in the United States of America

978-1-941663-61-5
978-1-941663-62-2 Kindle
978-1-941663-63-9 ePub

Introduction

The message of salvation is at the center of the Christian faith. It is proclaimed throughout Scripture, and a summary of it is found in one of the most famous verses of the Bible: "For God so loved the world that he gave his only Son, that whoever believes in him should not perish but have eternal life" (John 3:16). In a remarkably short space, this verse covers key themes connected with the message of salvation.

The first of these themes is God's love for mankind. This is at the root of our salvation. God loves us, and *how much* he loves us is indicated by the second theme.

When Scripture says that God gave his only Son, it refers to Jesus Christ and the key events of his life—particularly his death on the cross. God didn't just give his Son to be born among men—he gave him *to die on a cross* for our salvation. That's how much God loves us!

God does not force his gift of salvation upon us, however. We may choose to accept it—or not. Thus, a third theme in the verse refers to our response to God's initiative: if we place our faith in Jesus Christ, then we can receive the benefits that, in love, God wants to give us.

Chief among these benefits is that we will not "perish" but have "eternal life." This points to our eternal destiny beyond this life: we could perish in the sense of being eternally separated from God or we could have eternal life by being united with him forever in heaven.

The verse thus proceeds through several stages, from God's love for mankind to his giving his only Son, to our subsequent response, and finally to the consequences this will have for our eternal destiny.

It is a rich and beautiful text that contains much to be unpacked. That is what this book is about, for this verse was never meant to stand on its own. St. John was writing for people who were already familiar with the concept of salvation and its associated themes.

Today, many people have a passing familiarity with some of these themes, but there is much more to say, and there are many questions that people ask. Over the course of the centuries, scholars have devoted much thought and study to what Scripture reveals about God, his love, and the theme of salvation.

In this book, we will draw from the fruits of these centuries of study and reflection to provide twenty answers to key questions on the topic of salvation—a topic that is vital to all of us.

1. Why do I need to be saved?

We all need to be saved because of sin. That's what we need to be saved *from*.

People today sometimes hesitate to use the word *sin*. For some people, this word is a reminder of a religious upbringing that they would rather forget. For others, it's a strong word—one that can come across as intimidating. But regardless of how we feel about the word, the reality of sin is all around us.

We all know this. It doesn't matter whether one is religious or secular, liberal or conservative. All human beings have an innate recognition that something is wrong with the world, that people do things that they should not, and that we do wrong.

It doesn't matter who you are: Think about the things in this world that make you angry—things like cruelty, injustice, and indifference to the suffering of others. Every one of us can become morally outraged when we encounter these things in their pure, unadulterated forms.

We also have an inner sense—our conscience—that is meant to warn us when we are about to do something wrong, or that makes us feel ashamed when we have done wrong.

Regardless of what you call it, sin is a reality that is in the world and within us as well.

We also sense that sin must have consequences. If there is justice in the world, then ultimately, people can't simply get away with doing wrong.

It's easy to sense this when we consider evil written large—horrible conflicts that have killed millions, examples of genocide, or cases of ethnic cleansing. The people who cause these things simply cannot be allowed to get away with them! If there is justice in the world, then they must somehow, someday, be called to account.

Yet, we know that there are people who committed horrible crimes and seemed to get away with them entirely. Others may have suffered some consequences for what they did, but nowhere near enough, given the horrors they committed. Dictators, terrorists, and mass murderers—without seeming to repent or express the least remorse for what they have done—have either died peacefully in bed or suffered only a fraction of what they did to others.

This shows us that justice is not always done in this life. Yet, our hearts tell us that there *should* be justice in the world; and so there is, but not always in this life. Christianity holds that, while villains may get away with their deeds for a time, they will ultimately have to stand before their Creator and be accountable to him for what they have done.

This opens up a new perspective. Thus far we have been looking at evil in terms of wrongs done by one person against another. But when we consider our sins with respect to God, we see that there is another dimension.

Everything we have, every ability, talent, and aptitude, is a gift from God, and that means every time we sin, we misuse one of God's gifts. Sin thus involves an offense against God, a failure to love him and honor him by using his gifts properly.

Because our sins aren't just against our fellow men, but against our infinitely good, all-holy, and eternal Creator, they carry a special gravity—one that can have eternal consequences. This adds a special urgency to our need for salvation.

When our consciences tell us that we have done wrong, and when our sense of justice tells us that we will be held accountable for what we have done, we naturally desire mercy. Our hearts call out for it. This is true both when we think of the wrongs we have done against other people and when we realize that they are offenses against God. Fortunately, in both cases, mercy, or salvation from the consequences of our sins, is available.

The human heart thus contains powerful intuitions that form the backdrop to the drama of salvation: the intuitions that sin is real, that there is justice, and so sin has consequences in this life or the next, and that mercy or salvation is available for those who repent.

The Christian faith acknowledges these intuitions of the heart and the realities to which they point. It recognizes the realities of sin, justice, and salvation— and the importance they have for all of us.

2. What is original sin?

The sin and suffering that we see around us in the world today are not new. They have been with us since the beginning of human history. At their root is a concept that the Church refers to as *original sin*.

The *Catechism of the Catholic Church* (CCC) states, "The doctrine of original sin is, so to speak, the 'reverse side' of the Good News that Jesus is the Savior of all men, that all need salvation and that salvation is offered to all through Christ" (CCC 389).

Genesis 1 and 2 depict God creating mankind in a state that was "very good" (Gen. 1:31). In this original state, God and man lived in harmony. "As long as he remained in the divine intimacy, man would not have to suffer or die. The inner harmony of the human person, the harmony between man and woman, and finally the harmony between the first couple and all creation, comprised the state called 'original justice'" (CCC 376).

But man turned away from this union with God through the first sin, which Genesis depicts as the act of eating the forbidden fruit. "The account of the fall in Genesis 3 uses figurative language, but affirms a primeval event, a deed that took place at the beginning of the history of man. Revelation gives us the certainty of faith that the whole of human history is marked by the original fault freely committed by our first parents" (CCC 390).

If Adam and Eve had remained in original justice and divine, intimacy then they would have been able to pass this state on to their descendants. However, having lost this state through sin, they were unable to pass it on, and so all human beings today are born deprived of original holiness and justice. Thus, we are all said to be born in original sin.

However, this does not mean that we are personally guilty of Adam's sin or that God holds us accountable for what Adam did. For us, original sin refers to the state in which we are born without original righteousness. "Original sin is called 'sin' only in an analogical sense: It is a sin 'contracted' and not 'committed'—a state and not an act" (CCC 404). "Original sin does not have the character of a personal fault in any of Adam's descendants. It is a deprivation of original holiness and justice" (CCC 405).

The situation is like that of a rich man who gambles away his fortune and thus is unable to pass it on to his children. It is the gambler who is personally at fault, not his children, but the children experience the poverty that his actions brought about.

In the same way, God gave our first parents an abundance of spiritual riches that they lost through their own folly. The fault was theirs, not ours, but we are still born in spiritual poverty and out of union with God.

Human nature has not been totally corrupted and still retains many elements of the goodness that God endowed it with in the beginning, but original sin has had dramatic consequences for human nature: "It is wounded in the natural powers proper to it, subject to ignorance, suffering, and the dominion of death, and inclined to sin—an inclination to evil that is called concupiscence" (CCC 405).

The inclination to sin, or concupiscence, is particularly important, because it leads us to commit our own faults, through personal sin.

3. What is personal sin?

In contrast to original sin, personal sin represents the sins that we individually commit and for which we are personally responsible.

We all have a general sense of what personal sin is— that it involves doing something wrong, something evil, something we should not do. However, theologians have studied the concept, and the Church has a refined understanding of what sin is.

Put in general terms, sin is "an abuse of the freedom that God gives to created persons so that they are capable of loving him and loving one another" (CCC 387). Stated another way, it is "an offense against reason, truth, and right conscience; it is failure in genuine love for God and neighbor caused by a perverse attachment to certain goods" (CCC 1849).

In other words, we can become so attached to various good things—like pleasure, possessions, or popularity—that we make choices that put these things above the love we should have for God and our fellow human beings. When we do this, we sin.

All sin involves an unloving choice based on disordered desire, or concupiscence.

Originally, this word referred to any intense form of human desire, but in Christian thought it has taken on a special meaning. "St. John distinguishes three kinds of covetousness or concupiscence: lust of the flesh, lust of the eyes, and pride of life (1 John 2:16)" (CCC 2514). This triple concupiscence subjugates man "to the pleasures of the senses, covetousness for earthly goods, and self-assertion, contrary to the dictates of reason" (CCC 377).

When disordered desire leads us into making un-loving choices, the resulting sin will be one of two types: mortal or venial.

The first type is known as mortal sin because it pro-duces spiritual death. It destroys the virtue of charity in our hearts, charity being the supernatural love of God that unites us to him spiritually. By being sepa-rated from God in this way, mortal sin puts us in a state of spiritual death.

"For a sin to be mortal, three conditions must to-gether be met: Mortal sin is sin whose object is grave matter and which is also committed with full knowl-edge and deliberate consent" (CCC 1857).

The first of these conditions means that the sin must involve a matter that is grave in nature. "Grave matter is specified by the Ten Commandments, correspond-ing to the answer of Jesus to the rich young man: 'Do not kill, Do not commit adultery, Do not steal, Do not bear false witness, Do not defraud, Honor your father and your mother' (Mark 10:19)" (CCC 1858).

In principle, a sin against any one of the Ten Commandments can involve grave matter, though not all do so in practice. For example, stealing a few dollars from a multimillionaire is not likely to harm him in a grave way and so is unlikely to be grave matter. However, stealing the same amount of money from a starving homeless person might well do grave harm and so be grave matter. In the same way, failing to send a birthday card to a parent likely wouldn't do grave harm, but failing to provide your parents the basic care they need in old age could.

Some sins automatically involve grave matter. This is the case anytime an innocent human being is killed and any time an act of adultery is committed.

If grave matter is present, there are still two other conditions that need to be fulfilled for a sin to be mortal. "Mortal sin requires full knowledge and complete consent. It presupposes knowledge of the sinful character of the act, of its opposition to God's law. It also implies a consent sufficiently deliberate to be a personal choice" (CCC 1859).

Various factors can diminish or remove the knowledge and consent needed for a sin to be mortal. "Unintentional ignorance can diminish or even remove the imputability of a grave offense. . . . The promptings of feelings and passions can also diminish the voluntary and free character of the offense, as can external pressures or pathological disorders" (CCC 1860).

When a person commits a sin and one or more of the conditions needed for it to be mortal are not present, the result is a venial sin (CCC 1862). Venial sins offend and wound the virtue of charity, but they do not destroy it, which is why they are not mortal (CCC 1855). They thus do not lead to spiritual death.

When our sins are mortal, however, our souls are in jeopardy, and we are in urgent need of God's grace.

4. What is grace?

Looked at one way, grace is the antidote to sin. It is what God provides us to overcome both original and personal sin.

"Grace is favor, the free and undeserved help that God gives us to respond to his call to become children of God, adoptive sons, partakers of the divine nature and of eternal life" (CCC 1996).

We need grace because of the condition of spiritual poverty that we are born into as a result of original sin. In this state of separation from God, wounded human nature will not allow us to seek God and come to him. He must take the initiative by seeking us and giving us the help we need to freely choose him. Thus, Jesus tells us, "No one can come to me unless the Father who sent me draws him" (John 6:44).

Fortunately, God wants all men to have this opportunity. He "desires all men to be saved and to come to the knowledge of the truth" (1 Tim. 2:4), and so he offers all men the grace necessary to be saved (CCC 1260).

God did not have to do this. He does it freely, out of his love for all men, and we must freely choose whether or not to respond to his grace and accept his love. "God's free initiative demands man's free response, for God has created man in his image by conferring on him, along with freedom, the power to know him and love him. The soul only enters freely into the communion of love. God immediately touches and directly moves the heart of man. He has placed in man a longing for truth and goodness that only he can satisfy" (CCC 2002).

The particular helps that God gives us at certain moments in life—helps to come to him, to do good, or to resist sin—are known as *actual graces* (CCC 2000). They can take many forms. When someone preaches the gospel and we are moved to respond, that is a grace. When we see someone in need and are moved to help, that is a grace. And when our conscience warns us that something we are about to do is wrong, that also is a grace.

Actual graces appear at particular moments in our lives, but there is another kind of grace, which remains with us over the course of time. This is known as *sanctifying grace*.

"Sanctifying grace is the gratuitous gift of his life that God makes to us; it is infused by the Holy Spirit into the soul to heal it of sin and to sanctify it. Sanctifying grace makes us 'pleasing to God'" (CCC 2023-2024).

When a person has sanctifying grace, he is said to be in a state of grace. In this state, he is united with God spiritually and said to be in God's friendship. If he dies in the state of grace, he will go to heaven (though he may need to be purified first in purgatory).

When we come to God and are saved and justified, God gives us the theological virtues of faith, hope, and charity (CCC 1991). Of these, charity is the most important (1 Cor. 13:13). It is the virtue "by which we love God above all things for his own sake, and our neighbor as ourselves for the love of God" (CCC 1822).

Charity always accompanies sanctifying grace, and when one is eliminated, so is the other. This is why mortal sin "results in the loss of charity and the privation of sanctifying grace, that is, of the state of grace. If it is not redeemed by repentance and God's forgiveness, it causes exclusion from Christ's kingdom and the eternal death of hell" (CCC 1861).

In addition to sanctifying grace, God also gives us additional gifts of grace to help us live the Christian life and be of service to others.

Therefore, our salvation is entirely a product of God's grace: from the graces that lead us to turn to him; to the state of grace in which we are saved; to the graces that he gives us to live the Christian life; to help others, and to bring them to him as well.

5. How can I be saved?

The teachings of Christ are rich and can be explored in great depth, but a basic understanding of how we can be saved can be summarized in a very simple way—so simple that even a child can grasp it.

The number of things that the Bible says are needed for salvation is actually quite small, and we can summarize the basics this way: To come to God and be saved, you need to repent, have faith, and be baptized. If you commit mortal sin, you need to repent, have faith, and go to confession.

We can show each of these things from the Bible:

- The need to repent is shown by the fact that, right at the beginning of his ministry, Jesus began preaching the gospel, saying, "repent, and believe in the gospel" (Mark 1:14-15).

- The need for faith is shown when the author of the letter to the Hebrews writes that "without faith it is impossible to please him. For whoever would draw near to God must believe that he exists and that he rewards those who seek him" (Heb. 11:6).

- And the need for baptism is shown when St. Peter flatly tells us, "Baptism . . . now saves you" (1 Pet. 3:21).

So that's what you need to do if you want to come to God and be saved: Repent, have faith, and be baptized. If you do these things, you'll be in a state of grace, and as long as you remain in a state of grace, you'll go to heaven.

But we still have free will, and we can still turn our backs on God. Thus, St. Paul warns some of his readers that, if they have accepted a false gospel, then they have "fallen away from grace" (Gal. 5:4).

St. Paul is very clear about the possibility of committing mortal sin. He tells us, "Do not be deceived; neither the immoral, nor idolaters, nor adulterers, nor homosexuals, nor thieves, nor the greedy, nor drunkards, nor revilers, nor robbers will inherit the kingdom of God" (1 Cor. 6:9-10).

The fact that he warns against being deceived indicates that this is the kind of thing people could deceive themselves about: They could think that it's possible to be saved while still committing mortal sin.

Jesus also warned against mortal sin. When he was asked, "Teacher, what good deed must I do, to have eternal life?" he replied, "If you would enter life, keep the commandments." He then went on to quote fundamental moral principles: "You shall not kill, You shall not commit adultery, You shall not steal, You shall not bear false witness, Honor your father and mother, and, You shall love your neighbor as yourself" (Matt. 19:16-19).

To turn away from God and commit mortal sin is to do the opposite of repenting. Mortal sin cancels repentance and thus undoes one of the three things we need to be saved, and so it costs us salvation. As a result, when we fall into mortal sin, we need to turn back to God—to repent again and restore that condition. We also need to have faith—in Christ and in his Church.

Just as we need repentance, faith, and the sacrament of baptism to be saved the first time, we also need repentance, faith, and a sacrament to return to a state of salvation. But the sacrament is different. Scripture indicates that there is only "one baptism" (Eph. 4:5), and so instead of being baptized again, we need to go to confession (see Question 11, "What is confession?").

There is, of course, much more that can be said about salvation, but this summarizes the basic themes that Scripture stresses.

6. How should we understand the key concepts connected with salvation?

Once you go beyond a basic explanation of how to be saved and start studying the subject in more depth, you encounter a set of terms that are unfamiliar to most modern readers—terms like *redemption, atonement, sanctification,* and *justification.*

What do these terms mean, and how do they relate to more familiar terms like *forgiveness* and *salvation*?

All of these are ways of describing the things God provides for us as part of the overall process of salvation. Each term calls to mind a slightly different notion though some of these notions have been forgotten in contemporary English.

A good example is the word *forgiveness*. We use this word all the time today. Since we all make mistakes, we all need forgiveness—and not just from God but from each other. We thus have a good sense of what forgiveness is though most of us would be at a loss to define it precisely or say where it comes from.

In the New Testament, the word for forgiveness (*aphesis*) came from a root that meant "to send off," "to release," or "to let go." When applied in a religious context, it referred to releasing or letting go the guilt that a person had acquired by sinning. This guilt was often pictured as a debt, which is why in Matthew's version of the Our Father, Jesus teaches us to pray, "forgive us our debts, as we also have forgiven our debtors" (Matt. 6:12).

We also use the term *save* a great deal today, as when we hear news stories about people being saved from one calamity or another. We don't use the term *salvation* as often in nonreligious contexts, but it conveys the same basic idea. The Greek word for the concept (*sōtēria*) comes from a root that means "to make safe." By saving us from our sins, God makes us safe from their consequences. He rescues us from what would otherwise happen. (Incidentally, this same Greek word gives us the name for the branch of theology that studies salvation, *soteriology*).

Occasionally, we also use the word *redeem* outside of a religious context, as when we talk about a person redeeming something that they have put in hock at a pawnshop. Here the basic idea is of buying back what had been sold to the pawn dealer. The Greek word for redemption (*apolutrōsis*) carries a similar meaning, though in the ancient world it was used to refer to buying back a slave or a person who had been taken captive in war (and thus likely to be made a slave).

In a religious context, the Greek word referred to God redeeming people from various dangers, including slavery to sin. Jesus is referred to as the Redeemer of mankind because, by dying on the cross, he performed a sacrifice that paid the debt of our sins and thus bought mankind back from the consequences of its sins. St. Paul refers to this when he says, "you were bought with a price. So glorify God in your body" (1 Cor. 6:20).

In English, the word *atonement* came from the idea of creating harmony between two parties and thus making them "at one" with each other. This term is often used to refer to what Jesus provided for us by his death on the cross, thus bringing about harmony between God and man.

The term *sanctification* is not common today outside of a religious context. The Greek term (*hagiasmos*) comes from a root that means "to make holy." When God sanctifies us, he makes us holy.

Justification is also a term that is not common in contemporary English, and it requires a little care to understand it. The Greek word (*dikaiōsis*) comes from a root that means "to make right" or "to make just," though this can be understood in more than one way. In some contexts, it can refer to declaring someone in the right, in which case it can mean things like "acquit" or "vindicate," but it can also have other uses, which we will discuss later.

One thing that is important to realize is the relationship between justification and righteousness. These terms are closely linked, though this isn't obvious in English. The way our language developed, we didn't end up with a verb meaning "to make righteous," and so the verb *to justify* is used instead.

In Greek, the terms for righteousness (*dikaiosunē*) and justification (*dikaiōsis*) are so clearly related that it is obvious we are dealing with a single underlying concept of rightness/justness. So it is important to remember, whenever reading about righteousness and justification, that the two concepts are somewhat interchangeable.

That is, in fact, something that it is important to realize about all these terms. They all describe ways in which God works in our lives, but the Bible often uses them in an overlapping, interchangeable manner, and we shouldn't build walls between the concepts.

7. How should we answer the question, "Have you been saved?"

Our Evangelical friends often use the question, "Have you been saved?" when they are evangelizing, and Catholics are sometimes unsure how to respond. The question presupposes a certain understanding of salvation that is unique to Protestantism and it's not obvious to non-Protestants how best to answer.

The most basic thing those asking the question are after is whether you have a relationship with God and have received his saving grace.

If you're a Catholic, you have. You have a relationship with God by virtue of your repentance, faith, and baptism, and by these you received his saving grace. Consequently, if you don't have time to discuss the matter further, you could simply say yes to the question and leave it at that.

However, there's more to the subject, and that presents you with an opportunity to help your Evangelical friend gain a deeper understanding of the Bible's teaching on salvation.

For example, the question, "Have you been saved?" envisions salvation as an accomplished event that lies in your past, as something that has already happened.

Sometimes the Bible speaks of salvation this way. For example, in his letter to the Ephesians, St. Paul twice tells his readers that "by grace you have been saved" (Eph. 2:5, 8). That speaks of salvation as something that occurred in the believers' past.

However, this is not the only way the Bible speaks of salvation. For example, St. Paul elsewhere tells his readers to "work out your own salvation with fear and trembling" (Phil. 2:12). And St. Peter tells his readers, "As the outcome of your faith you obtain the salvation of your souls" (1 Pet. 1:9). The Greek word here translated as "obtain" is in the present tense, which in the original Greek suggests ongoing action. Both of these texts speak of salvation as something that is ongoing—something that is still being worked out and obtained.

The Bible also speaks of salvation as a future event. In his letter to the Romans, Paul tells the reader that "salvation is nearer to us now than when we first believed" (Rom. 13:11). And in his first letter to the Corinthians, St. Paul talks about how some people "will be saved, but only as through fire," and how a certain type of believer needs to be disciplined now "that his spirit may be saved in the day of the Lord Jesus" (1 Cor. 3:15, 5:5).

These passages speak of salvation as a future event. So while we can speak of salvation as something occurring in the past, the New Testament reveals that it is also something happening in our lives now—in the present—and that it is something that has yet to happen in the future.

If you want to help your Evangelical friend gain a deeper understanding of the Bible's teaching on salvation, you might answer the question "Have you been saved?" by saying, "I have been saved, I am being saved, and I hope to be saved."

The same is true of other aspects of salvation. They also have already been accomplished in one sense but not in others.

For example, the Bible sometimes refers to our redemption as an accomplished fact (Eph. 1:7; Col. 1:13) and sometimes as a future event (Rom. 8:23; Eph. 1:14, 4:30). It does the same thing with forgiveness, speaking of it as past (Eph. 1:7, 4:32; Col. 1:14, 3:13) and as ongoing (Matt. 6:12; Jas. 5:15; 1 John 1:19).

Our Protestant friends sometimes speak of justification as something occurring in the past and sanctification as something that is ongoing, but these also have more than one dimension. Thus Scripture sometimes speaks of justification, or the reception of righteousness from God, as past (Rom. 5:12; 1 Cor. 6:11) and as something ongoing or in the future (Rom. 2:13, 3:20; Gal. 5:5). Similarly, it speaks of sanctification sometimes as an accomplished fact (1 Cor. 6:11; Heb. 10:10) and sometimes as something still happening (1 Thess. 4:1, 3, 5:23; Heb. 2:11, 10:14).

This shows us that we shouldn't conceive of any of these ways God works in our lives as exclusively past, present, or future. God may do some things in our lives in a "once for all" way (like when he seals our souls in the sacraments of baptism, confirmation, and holy orders; see CCC 698), but the things we have covered don't work that way. They have a beginning in our lives when we first come to God, but they continue to unfold over the course of our lives thereafter.

8. Why did Jesus die on the cross?

From one perspective, Jesus died on the cross because he began a popular movement that the Jewish authorities believed would initiate a rebellion against the Roman rulers of Judea and lead to a disastrous war (John 11:47-53). Consequently, they arrested Jesus, handed him over to the Roman governor, and demanded his execution. The governor then complied, using crucifixion, which was commonly used for the enemies of the Roman Empire.

From his own perspective, Jesus died on the cross because he recognized this was a key part of the mission on which his Father had sent him. Jesus accepted it, even though he could have avoided it had he chosen (Matt. 26:53-54; John 10:17-18).

But why was it his Father's plan for him to die on a cross? Crucifixion was an exceptionally cruel form of execution, and the idea of a crucified Son of God was a startling one to people in the ancient world. St. Paul described the message of the cross as "a stumbling block to Jews and folly to Gentiles" (1 Cor. 1:23).

What was happening in this surprising sequence of events?

We gain insight from perhaps the most famous verse in the New Testament, John 3:16: "For God so loved the world that he gave his only Son, that whoever believes in him should not perish but have eternal life." In a few strokes, this verse encapsulates the basic Christian message. God loves us, and so he used Jesus' death on the cross to save us from eternal death (separation from God, hell) so that we might have eternal life (union with God, heaven).

But why would God choose crucifixion, or any form of execution, to be the means by which this would happen? Some have pointed out that it was prophesied that the Messiah would suffer and thereby save others (Isa. 53), but this doesn't answer the question of why God chose this means in the first place.

The answer seems to be that God was drawing on a theme that first-century Jews, and others, would have understood—the theme of sacrifice. By willingly going to the cross, Jesus sacrifices his own life to save others, and sacrifice was something everybody in the ancient world understood. It was the universal means by which God or the gods were worshipped.

In a sacrifice, people would bring a gift—often an animal—and offer it on an altar. The sacrifice could either be offered as a gesture of apology for having sinned or as an act of worship and reverence. Either way, the gift of the sacrifice was meant to cultivate good relations with heaven.

Thus, though the crucifixion of the Son of God might be a surprising way of offering a sacrifice, it was something that, when explained, people could understand: Jesus was presenting himself as a sacrifice on our behalf. Indeed, he was the sacrifice to which all other Jewish sacrifices ultimately pointed, "for it is impossible that the blood of bulls and goats should take away sins" (Heb. 10:4).

In choosing the crucifixion as the means of our salvation, God drew on one theme that had particular meaning for Jews—the theme of Passover. At the founding of their nation, God led them out of slavery in Egypt through the sacrifice of lambs at the time of Passover, when God's wrath passed over the Israelites.

Now Jesus, "the Lamb of God" (John 1:29, 36), was sacrificed at Passover (John 19:14-16), so that God's wrath might pass over us, and we might be led out of enslavement to sin. Thus St. Paul can say that "Christ, our paschal lamb, has been sacrificed" (1 Cor. 5:7).

Could God have chosen another way to bring about the salvation of the world? Yes. He is omnipotent, and he could have redeemed mankind in any way he chose. According to the common theological opinion, he could have simply forgiven our sins and saved us without any earthly sacrifice (see St. Thomas Aquinas, *Summa Theologiae* III:46:2, reply to obj. 3).

Nevertheless, by choosing this means of accomplishing the redemption of man, God drew on themes that could be understood by men. The impulse to sacrifice is found in cultures all over the world and is innate to human nature, providing a way for people everywhere to understand what Christ did for us.

The theme of the Passover lamb was of particular meaning to the Jewish people, and so God accomplished the redemption in a way that built on what he had already established among his chosen people.

He also communicated important lessons to us. One is just how serious our sins are, given that it took the death of the Son of God to atone for them. Even more fundamentally, though, he showed us just how much he loves us in spite of our sins. "God shows his love for us in that while we were yet sinners Christ died for us" (Rom. 5:8; cf. CCC 604).

9. What is a sacrament?

Every religion has certain rites and ceremonies that it regards as sacred. Sometimes, these have been referred to as the "mysteries" of the religion (from the Greek word *mustērion*) or as its "sacraments" (from the Latin word *sacramentum*).

The fact that these are a human universal, found in every religion, in every culture, means that they correspond to something that is part of human nature. It makes sense, then, that God would make use of them when interacting with mankind.

Therefore, we see in Judaism what Catholic authors have sometimes referred to as the *sacraments of the Mosaic Law* or the *sacraments of the Old Law*. These include rites such as the eating of the Passover lamb, the sacrifices offered at the temple, circumcision, and various washings for purification that were required by the Mosaic Law (see Exod. 12; Lev. 1-7, 12:3, 14:8-9).

From a Christian perspective, these rites not only played a role in their own time, they also pointed forward to the Christian age. As a result of the coming of Christ, they have now been fulfilled and superseded, so Christians do not observe them (see Col. 2:16-17).

However, the principle that led God to institute these rites for the Jewish people before Christ remains part of human nature, and so Christianity has its own sacred rites and ceremonies.

Some of these correspond in a special way to the Jewish ceremonies that preceded them. For example, baptism is the rite by which one becomes a Christian, and it thus corresponds to circumcision, by which men became Jews. St. Paul even refers to baptism as "the circumcision of Christ," or the Christian equivalent of circumcision (Col. 2:11-13; cf. CCC 527). Since baptism involves a washing with water, it also corresponds in a way to the various ceremonial washings used in Judaism.

Similarly, as we saw, the New Testament identifies Christ as "the Lamb of God" (John 1:29, 36), and St.

Paul specifically identifies him as the Christian equivalent of the Passover lamb (1 Cor. 5:7). Jesus' death on the cross as an offering for our sins fulfills the sin offerings that were offered at the Jewish temple (Heb. 10:1-10). Consuming the Eucharist, the body and blood of Christ (Matt. 26:26-28), which makes present the sacrifice of the cross, thus corresponds to the eating of the Passover lamb and the Old Testament sin offerings.

Although there is a rich variety of rites and ceremonies used in Christianity, certain ones have a special place and are referred to as the *sacraments of the New Law* or the *sacraments of the New Covenant* established by Christ.

Used this way, the word *sacrament* refers to "efficacious signs of grace, instituted by Christ and entrusted to the Church, by which divine life is dispensed to us. The visible rites by which the sacraments are celebrated signify and make present the graces proper to each sacrament. They bear fruit in those who receive them with the required dispositions" (CCC 1131).

Over the course of time, the Church has discerned that there are seven such sacraments: baptism (Matt. 28:19), confirmation (Acts 8:14-17; Heb. 6:2), the Eucharist (1 Cor. 10:16), confession (John 20:21-23), the anointing of the sick (Mark 6:13; James 5:14-15), holy orders (Acts 13:2-3; 2 Tim. 1:6), and matrimony (CCC 1612-1617).

In contrast to the rites that were part of the Old Testament, the sacraments of the New Covenant actually impart the graces that they signify. Each serves as a visible sign of the invisible graces that it imparts.

This twofold nature of the sacraments corresponds to the twofold nature of man: We are not simply created spirits, like the angels. By nature, human beings are composed of both body and spirit. As a result, God imparts spiritual graces to us through visible, bodily signs (ST III:61:1).

In his ministry, Jesus frequently performed miracles through sensible signs like the spoken word (Mark 4:39; John 11:43-44) and the laying on of hands (Mark 8:23-25; Luke 4:40). This same principle is at work in the sacraments that Jesus established for his Church.

Different sacraments convey different graces. For example, the anointing of the sick is directed in a special way toward healing, holy orders is directed toward empowering men for ordained ministry, and matrimony is directed toward empowering couples to live the married life.

Two sacraments—baptism and confession—are specially directed toward taking a person who is not in a state of grace and placing him in a state of sanctifying grace, thus producing the forgiveness of sins (CCC 1279, 1486). Some other sacraments, like the anointing of the sick, may be able to do this in special circumstances (CCC 1532), but baptism and confirmation do this as one of their primary, ordinary functions. As a result, these two play special roles in the ordinary process of salvation.

10. What is baptism?

Baptism is the sacrament by which a person becomes a Christian. Jesus stressed the role of baptism in making disciples when he gave the Great Commission to his disciples, telling them, "Go therefore and make disciples of all nations, baptizing them in the name of the Father and of the Son and of the Holy Spirit" (Matt. 28:19).

The parallel account in Mark stresses the role of baptism in salvation. There Jesus says, "Go into all the world and preach the gospel to the whole creation. He who believes and is baptized will be saved; but he who does not believe will be condemned" (Mark 16:15-16).

The same theme is picked up by other New Testament texts (John 3:5; Acts 2:38, 22:16; Rom. 6:4; 1 Cor. 12:13; Gal. 3:27; Col. 2:12).

We have already seen that St. Peter declares bluntly that "baptism . . . now saves you" (1 Pet. 3:21).

Some might wonder how the application of water to a person's body could save him, but we have also seen the sacramental principle in which God uses a visible sign, like water, to convey a spiritual grace. It isn't the fact that water makes a person physically cleaner that saves him. It is the spiritual side of baptism that accomplishes this. Thus, Peter clarifies that baptism saves "not as a removal of dirt from the body but as an appeal to God for a clear conscience, through the resurrection of Jesus Christ" (ibid.).

Normally, baptism is performed by an ordained minister, but in cases of necessity any person can baptize another (CCC 1256).

Baptism makes a permanent change in the soul of the person who receives it, and so it can be received validly only once. In contrast to the many Jewish washings, St. Paul stresses that among Christians there is "one baptism" (Eph. 4:5; cf. CCC 1280).

Though one can administer baptism by immersion, it can also be administered by pouring water on the head. This corresponds to the image of the Holy Spirit being "poured out" on the disciples (Acts 2:33, 10:45).

History reveals that baptism was administered in different ways from the very beginning. The first-century Christian document known as the *Didache* (*DID-ah-KAY*) is a witness to this, stating, "baptize into the name of the Father, and of the Son, and of the Holy Spirit, in living [i.e., running] water. But if you have not living water, baptize in other water; and if you cannot in cold, in warm. But if you have not either, pour out water three times upon the head in the name of Father and Son and Holy Spirit" (*Didache* 7).

By giving the recipient sanctifying grace, baptism forgives both original sin and personal sin. It does not, however, remove the disordered desire—or concupiscence—that we have inherited on account of original sin. As a result, we must continue to struggle against sin through the course of the Christian life and thus grow in holiness (CCC 1426).

"The fruit of Baptism, or baptismal grace, is a rich reality that includes forgiveness of original sin and all personal sins, birth into the new life by which man becomes an adoptive son of the Father, a member of Christ and a temple of the Holy Spirit. By this very fact the person baptized is incorporated into the Church, the Body of Christ, and made a sharer in the priesthood of Christ" (CCC 1279).

These graces are the reason that the Church baptizes small children. "Born with a fallen human nature and tainted by original sin, children also have need of the new birth in baptism to be freed from the power of darkness and brought into the realm of the freedom of the children of God, to which all men are called. The sheer gratuitousness of the grace of salvation is particularly manifest in infant baptism. The Church and the parents would deny a child the priceless grace of becoming a child of God were they not to confer Baptism shortly after birth" (CCC 1250).

By identifying baptism as "the circumcision of Christ" (Col. 2:11-12), or the Christian equivalent of circumcision, St. Paul establishes a principle that supports the baptism of infants. In Judaism, circumcision was applied both to adult converts and to the children of believers in order to make them partakers of the Old Covenant. In Christianity, baptism is applied both to adult converts and to the children of believers to make them participants in the New Covenant.

"The practice of infant Baptism is an immemorial tradition of the Church. There is explicit testimony to this practice from the second century on, and it is quite possible that, from the beginning of the apostolic preaching, when whole 'households' received baptism, infants may also have been baptized" (CCC 1252; cf. Acts 16:15, 33, 18:8; 1 Cor. 1:16; see also Jimmy Akin, *The Fathers Know Best*, ch. 40).

Although God has promised to give his grace through baptism, and although we are obliged to seek his grace through the means that he has appointed, God is not bound to give his grace *only* through baptism. He has mercy on those who, through no fault of their own, are not baptized.

"With respect to children who have died without Baptism, the liturgy of the Church invites us to trust in God's mercy and to pray for their salvation" (CCC 1283).

Similarly, with adults, "those who die for the faith, those who are catechumens, and all those who, without knowing of the Church but acting under the inspiration of grace, seek God sincerely and strive to fulfill his will, are saved even if they have not been baptized" (CCC 1281).

For more on the sacrament of baptism, see CCC 1213-1284.

11. What is confession?

Confession is the sacrament by which we ordinarily are restored to a state of grace when we have committed mortal sin after baptism.

It is also sometimes referred to as the sacrament of reconciliation and the sacrament of penance (distinct from nonsacramental forms of penance).

The need for the sacrament of confession is based on the fact that, even after we have been baptized and entered a state of grace, we can commit mortal sin. Baptism does not remove temptations to sin, and we can use our free will knowingly and deliberately to commit acts that are gravely sinful. When this happens, we fulfill the conditions for mortal sin, and the spiritual life within us dies. We leave the state of grace.

Some in the Protestant community have denied this, claiming that when we first come to God and are saved, he forgives all our sins—past, present, and future—so even the sins we have not yet committed are forgiven.

There are no verses in Scripture that state this. In fact, there are passages that indicate the opposite.

One of them is the Lord's Prayer, in which Jesus teaches us to pray, "forgive us our sins, for we ourselves forgive everyone who is indebted to us" (Luke 11:4; cf. Matt. 6:12). Here, in the model Christian prayer, Jesus teaches us to pray for forgiveness on an ongoing basis. This means that we *need* forgiveness on an ongoing basis. As we commit new sins, we need to be forgiven for them.

There is even a condition attached: Jesus indicates that we need to take the same merciful attitude toward others that we want God to take toward us. This does not mean that we should never be angry with another person (cf. Eph. 4:26) or that we should forget the wrongs they have done to us or cease to be cautious around them in the future (cf. 2 Tim. 4:14-15), but it does mean that we should be willing to forgive them whenever they repent (Luke 17:3-4; cf. Matt. 18:21-22).

While prayer may be sufficient for the forgiveness of daily, venial sins, Jesus indicated that some sins are more serious, and a sacrament is involved in their forgiveness. Since baptism can be received only once, Christ instituted the sacrament of confession.

He did this just after he rose from the dead, when he came to his disciples and told them, "As the Father has sent me, even so I send you." Then he breathed on them, and said, "Receive the Holy Spirit. If you forgive the sins of any, they are forgiven; if you retain the sins of any, they are retained" (John 20:21-23).

Before this, God had sent Jesus to forgive sins on earth (Matt. 9:6), and the people glorified God "who had given such authority to men" (Matt. 9:8). But here Jesus shares this authority with his ministers by empowering them by the Holy Spirit to forgive or retain sins.

Of course, for a priest to know whether he is to forgive or retain a sin, he needs to know about the sin and whether we have repented of it. That means we need to go and tell him these things, and so we have the sacrament of confession, or penance.

"The sacrament of penance is a whole consisting in three actions of the penitent and the priest's absolution. The penitent's acts are repentance, confession or disclosure of sins to the priest, and the intention to make reparation and do works of reparation" (CCC 1491).

The last of these is needed because "many sins wrong our neighbor. One must do what is possible in order to repair the harm (e.g., return stolen goods, restore the reputation of someone slandered, pay compensation for injuries). Simple justice requires as much. But sin also injures and weakens the sinner himself, as well as his relationships with God and neighbor. Absolution takes away sin, but it does not remedy all the disorders sin has caused. Raised up from sin, the sinner must still recover his full spiritual health by doing something more to make amends for the sin" (CCC 1459).

Thus, "the confessor proposes the performance of certain acts of 'satisfaction' or 'penance' to be performed by the penitent in order to repair the harm caused by sin and to re-establish habits befitting a disciple of Christ" (CCC 1494).

"One who desires to obtain reconciliation with God and with the Church, must confess to a priest all the unconfessed grave sins he remembers after having carefully examined his conscience. The confession of venial faults, without being necessary in itself, is nevertheless strongly recommended by the Church" (CCC 1493).

Sometimes, through no fault of their own, people are not able to go to confession, and God makes provision for this. It is thus possible for people to be reconciled with God and to return to the state of grace through what is known as perfect contrition.

"Repentance (also called contrition) must be inspired by motives that arise from faith. If repentance arises from love of charity for God, it is called 'perfect' contrition" (CCC 1492). Perfect contrition "obtains forgiveness of mortal sins if it includes the firm resolution to have recourse to sacramental confession as soon as possible" (CCC 1452).

Thus, it is possible for a person to be reconciled with God even if they are not able to receive the sacrament at present.

Perfect contrition is an expression of God's willingness to forgive us no matter what we have done, as illustrated in the parable of the prodigal son (Luke 15:11-32). In this parable, a man starts as a genuine son of his father but leaves the family and lives a life of grave sin. In this state, he is described by his father as "dead," but when he returns, he is embraced by the father and described as being "alive again" (Luke 15:24). In the same way, we can be genuine sons of our Father in heaven but turn our back on him, becoming spiritually dead through mortal sin, and then return to him and be reconciled, being made spiritually alive again.

For more on the sacrament of confession, see CCC 1422-1498.

12. If Jesus died for our sins, why should we do penance?

The value of Christ's self-offering on the cross was infinite—more than enough to pay for all the sins of mankind. But it seems that, even after God has forgiven the eternal consequences of our sins and restored our relationship with him, he wants us to experience *some* negative consequences.

It's rather like the situation in a family. When a child misbehaves, there need to be consequences. If parents simply told the child that he's forgiven and never applied any discipline then the child would never learn his lesson. That's why children hear their parents say things like, "It's okay. I forgive you. But you're still grounded."

The Bible uses the image of parental discipline to express how God relates to us as his children. The book of Hebrews tells us that "the Lord disciplines him whom he loves, and chastises every son whom he receives" (Heb. 12:6). It also tells us that he "disciplines us for our good, that we may share his holiness" (Heb. 12:10).

So even when we've become children of God and been forgiven, God still disciplines us. He allows us to experience some consequences for our sins so that we may grow in holiness.

That's why we do penance. It's a way of embracing discipline, of learning to do it, to internalize it, and it builds strength and self-control for the future. If we learn how to say no to ourselves as part of penance, we'll be better able to say no to temptations in the future.

The idea that Christians shouldn't do penance because Christ died for their sins is not found in the Bible. In fact, Christ himself *expected* us to do penance.

At one point, Jesus was asked why his disciples did not fast—fasting being a form of penance—and he said that they would in the future. He compared himself to the bridegroom at a wedding and his disciples to the wedding guests. Jesus pointed out that it's not appropriate to fast at a wedding celebration, but he went on to say, "The days will come, when the bridegroom is taken away from them, and then they will fast in that day" (Mark 2:20).

He expected fasting, and thus penance, to be a regular part of Christian practice. That's why, in the Sermon on the Mount, he told the disciples, "when you fast, do not look dismal, like the hypocrites" (Matt. 6:16).

Notice that he doesn't say, "*if* you fast" but instead "*when* you fast." He *expects* us to fast, and he gives instructions on how to do it.

In the book of Acts, we see the early Christians putting this into practice. St. Paul's commission to missionary work occurred after he and other church leaders "were worshiping the Lord and fasting" (Acts 13:2), and later Paul appointed elders "in every church, with prayer and fasting" (Acts 14:23).

Fasting is also mentioned in early Christian writings outside the New Testament. For example, the *Didache* indicates that it was common for first-century Christians to fast twice a week. The *Didache* states, "And let not your fastings be with the hypocrites, for they fast on the second and the fifth day of the week [i.e., Monday and Thursday]; but keep your fast on the fourth and on the preparation day [i.e., Wednesday and Friday]" (*Didache* 8:1-2).

By voluntarily embracing fasting and other forms of penance, we embrace spiritual discipline that will, as the book of Hebrews says, help us grow in holiness. And that's one of the reasons why, even though Christ died for us, we still do penance.

Penance also provides us with an opportunity to express sorrow for our sins. We have an innate need to mourn when something tragic has occurred, and that includes our own sins.

The fact that God forgives our sins does not remove this need to mourn any more than the fact that a man's

44

wife may be in heaven means that he doesn't need to mourn her death.

Both sin and death are tragedies, and while forgiveness and salvation mean that they do not have the last word, we still need to grieve. To insist that a person not feel or show any grief for them would be unnatural and would short-circuit natural responses that God built into us. There is "a time to weep, and a time to laugh; a time to mourn, and a time to dance" (Eccles. 3:4).

13. What is justification?

In the most basic terms, justification is the act of making someone just or righteous.

This can be understood in different ways. In Luke's Gospel, a lawyer asks Jesus what he needs to do to inherit eternal life, and Jesus replies that he should love God and love his neighbor. But the lawyer, "desiring to justify himself, said to Jesus, 'And who is my neighbor?'" (Luke 10:29).

In this case, the lawyer wants to make himself just or righteous in the opinion *of others*. But in theology we aren't concerned with making people just or righteous in front of men but rather in front of God. We are seeking is *God's* declaration that we are just.

The problem is our sin. All of us have sin, so how can we be righteous before God? The answer is: only by his grace.

Because of what Christ did for us on the cross, God is willing to forgive our sins and make us just in spite of them. He, therefore, makes a gift to us of righteousness, or justification.

Although both Protestants and Catholics agree on this much, they tend to use the term *justification* somewhat differently.

In the Protestant community, the term *justification* is often used to refer to the event at the beginning of the Christian life in which God forgives us and makes us righteous, but righteousness is frequently understood as being purely legal in nature.

Frequently, our Protestant brethren conceive of justification in terms of a courtroom analogy, whereby God declares us righteous in a kind of legal fiction. In this view, even though we have committed sins, he attributes to us the righteousness of Christ so that our sins are covered over and—in terms of the divine court—we enjoy the same righteousness that Christ has. This means, it is sometimes said, that God "treats us just like Jesus."

This view contains elements of truth, but it is also problematic. One reason is that God continues to treat Christ differently than he treats us. Because of Christ's unique nature and role, God gave him "the name which is above every name, that at the name of Jesus every knee should bow, in heaven and on earth and under the earth" (Phil. 2:9-10).

God, therefore, does not treat us exactly like Jesus. He forgives our sins, but he doesn't give us each "the name above every name." We aren't all coequal with Christ. We are the subjects in Christ's kingdom, not the king.

In Catholic theology, the term *justification* is used to refer to two things: (1) the remission or forgiveness of sins and (2) the sanctification and renewal of the inner man (CCC 1989).

It thus includes the forgiveness of sins that is prominent in Protestant theologies of justification, but it goes beyond that, because the righteousness that God gives us in justification isn't merely a legal righteousness. It's a real, objective righteousness that sanctifies and renews us inwardly. It is what Catholics refer to as sanctifying grace (CCC 1266).

This is in keeping with Romans 6:6-7. In standard translations, this reads: "We know that our old self was crucified with [Christ] so that the sinful body might be destroyed, and we might no longer be enslaved to sin. For he who has died is freed from sin."

The last part of this, which says that one who has died "is freed" from sin, would be literally translated, "For he who has died *has been justified* from sin." The literal translation reveals how justification itself involves a liberation from sin so that we are no longer enslaved to it. The righteousness we receive in justification is thus not merely legal. It changes us so that we are *freed from sin.*

Although Protestants and Catholics use the word *justification* somewhat differently in this way, their views are closer than often supposed. While Protestants often do not include the sanctification and renewal of the inner man under the term *justification*, they do acknowledge that it is something God does at the beginning of the Christian life, at the same time as justification, but they refer to it by the term *sanctification*.

In Catholic theology, *justification* and *sanctification* are often used as synonyms, though they are also sometimes distinguished (cf. CCC 2001).

Catholic and Protestants thus can agree that, at the beginning of the Christian life, God forgives us and sanctifies and renews our inner being. We may draw different lines between the terms *justification* and *sanctification* in describing these realities, but we do not need to quarrel about words (2 Tim. 2:14, cf. 1 Tim. 6:4-5).

Something similar applies to what happens after God justifies us at the beginning of the Christian life. Both Protestants and Catholics agree that, under the influence of God's grace, we go on to perform good works (Eph. 2:10). As a result, we grow in righteousness and holiness over the course of the Christian life.

In Protestant terminology, this process is often referred to as *sanctification*, while in Catholic terminology it is often referred to as *justification* or growth in justice. As before, the two positions use different terminology but need not be understood as opposed in substance.

From a Catholic point of view, justification then refers both to the event at the beginning of the Christian life in which God forgives us and makes us righteous by the gift of sanctifying grace, and also to the growth in righteousness that occurs over the course of the Christian life.

14. Are we justified "by faith alone"?

For the last five hundred years, one of the most controversial claims has been that we are saved, or justified, "by faith alone." This claim is often made by our Protestant friends, but different groups of Protestants understand it in different ways.

For example, some Protestants would say that if we are saved by faith alone, then that means baptism has no role in our salvation. Others would disagree. For instance, Lutherans recognize that the Bible means what it says when it declares that "baptism now saves you" (1 Pet. 3:21). Moreover, Martin Luther—the man who popularized the "by faith alone" formula—was very firm about the role of baptism in salvation.

For example, in his *Small Catechism*, Luther wrote:

Q. What does baptism give? What good is it?
A. It gives the forgiveness of sins, redeems from death and the devil, gives eternal salvation to all who believe this, just as God's words and promises declare.

Despite the differences among Protestants about what "faith alone" means, one thing all agree on is the fact that you don't have to do any "good works" in order to come to God and be justified.

That is true, and the Catholic Church agrees. In fact, the Church teaches that it is not possible for one to do any supernaturally good works before justification, because before that point you do not have the virtue of charity, which is what makes such works possible.

When we repent and are justified, God puts the virtue of charity—or the supernatural love of God and neighbor—into our hearts (CCC 1991). This means that good works flow from justification. They are not something we need to do to attain state of grace. As the *Joint Declaration on the Doctrine of Salvation* puts it, "Good works—a Christian life lived in faith, hope and love—follow justification and are its fruits. When the justified live in Christ and act in the grace they receive, they bring forth, in biblical terms, good fruit" (JD 37).

In his letter to the Galatians, St. Paul refers to "faith working through love" (Gal. 5:6), and Catholic theologians have said that if this is the way you understand faith then the formula "by faith alone" can be given an acceptable meaning. Pope Benedict XVI said:

Luther's phrase "*faith alone*" is true, if it is not opposed to faith in charity, in love. . . . So it is that in the Letter to the Galatians, in which he primarily developed his teaching on justification, St. Paul speaks of faith that works through love (General Audience, November 19, 2008).

While the "faith alone" formula *can* be given an acceptable meaning, that doesn't mean that it's a good or natural way to express the Bible's teaching.

In fact, it is not the language of Scripture. St. Paul *never* uses this phrase. The only time it does appear in Scripture is in James 2, where the formula is rejected. St. James writes that "a man is justified by works and not by faith alone" (James 2:24).

This doesn't contradict what we've just said, because James is not speaking of the event where we first come to God and are justified. Instead, he's speaking of our later, ongoing growth in righteousness—and good works do contribute to that, as we cooperate with God's grace and grow in holiness.

Note that James refers to how Abraham was "justified by works, when he offered his son Isaac upon the altar" (James 2:21). This refers to an event in Genesis 22, long after he was reckoned righteous in Genesis 15, and still longer after he began following God in faith in Genesis 12 (see Gen. 12:1-4, 15:1-6; Heb. 11:1-2, 8-9; James 2:22-23).

This is another indication that justification is something that is an ongoing part of the Christian life.

Good works may not play a role in one's initial justification at the beginning of one's walk with God, but they do flow from this justification and play a role in one's ongoing justification or growth in righteousness.

Historically, in Catholic theology the word *faith* has been understood to mean "the theological virtue by which we believe in God and believe all that he has said and revealed to us, and that Holy Church proposes for our belief, because he is truth itself" (CCC 1814).

Understood in this way, faith separated from charity is not enough to save. As James explains, "faith without works is dead" (James 2:26), and so "when it is deprived of hope and love, faith does not fully unite the believer to Christ and does not make him a living member of his Body" (CCC 1815).

The fact that "faith" is often used to mean intellectual assent to the truths of the faith rather than "faith working through love," and the fact that the "faith alone" formula is rejected the one time that it is used in Scripture, mean that we need to be careful, because the formula is very easy to misunderstand.

15. What are "works of the law"?

St. Paul is clear that we do not achieve salvation through what he refers to as "works of the law." For example, in his letter to the Romans, Paul states, "we hold that a man is justified by faith apart from works of law" (Rom. 3:28).

It's clear what Paul means by "faith": He means faith in Jesus Christ. However, what does he mean by "works of the law"? If you look at the context closely, it turns out that he means something very specific.

The key is figuring out what law Paul is talking about. For the Jewish people, the most famous law is the Law of Moses, which is found in the first five books of the Bible.

This was the fundamental law of Judaism. It characterized Jews but not Gentiles. It required circumcision. Moreover, it was regarded as one of the main components of the Scriptures, along with the prophets. That's why the New Testament refers to the two principle components of the Jewish Scriptures as "the law and the prophets."

When we look at the contexts in which Paul talks about "works of the law," we find that this is the law Paul is discussing.

After saying that we are justified by faith apart from works of the law, Paul immediately asks, "Or is God the God of Jews only? Is he not the God of Gentiles also?" (Rom. 3:29). That tells us that the law in question is one that applies to Jews but not Gentiles, which is what the Mosaic Law does.

He then refers to circumcision, the most famous requirement of the Law of Moses, saying that God "will justify the circumcised on the ground of their faith and the uncircumcised through their faith" (Rom. 3:30).

Similarly, in Galatians, Paul raises the question of Jews and Gentiles and again says that "a man is not justified by works of the law but through faith in Jesus Christ" (Gal. 2:16).

Just before this, he referred to a time when he went to Jerusalem for a council with other early Christian leaders, and he noted that his traveling companion Titus was not required to undergo circumcision, even though he was a Greek (Gal. 2:1-10).

We read about this same event in Acts. It happened when "some men came down from Judea and were teaching the brethren, 'Unless you are circumcised according to the custom of Moses, you cannot be saved'" (Acts 15:1). The apostles and elders then held a council at which they reiterated the fact that Gentile Christians did not need to be circumcised and become Jews in order to be saved.

That's what Paul is talking about in Romans and Galatians when he contrasts faith in Christ with works of the law. He is stressing that you don't have to be circumcised, become a Jew, and obey the Mosaic Law to be saved.

Therefore, he tells his readers, "I testify again to every man who receives circumcision that he is bound to keep the whole law. You are severed from Christ, you who would be justified by the law; you have fallen away from grace. For through the Spirit, by faith, we wait for the hope of righteousness. For in Christ Jesus neither circumcision nor uncircumcision is of any avail, but faith working through love" (Gal. 5:3-6).

Unfortunately, though this issue had been settled as soon as St. Peter admitted Gentiles to the Church without circumcising them (Acts 10:1–11:18), the controversy lasted for some time in various places. Even after the council in Acts 15, some people in Galatia and Rome apparently hadn't gotten the word or hadn't taken it seriously enough.

That's why Paul writes to them and stresses that we are saved through our faith in Christ, not by obeying the Mosaic Law.

A careful reading of Paul's writings thus reveals that "works of the law" are actions that people thought they needed to do in order to obey the Law of Moses.

They're *not* the same thing as good works, which *are* part of the Christian life. In fact, Paul says that God created us "in Christ Jesus for good works, which God prepared beforehand, that we should walk in them" (Eph. 2:10).

16. What is merit?

The term *merit* (Latin, *meritum*) refers to a reward. By extension, it has also come to refer to actions that God chooses to reward. The doctrine of merit is thus the biblical doctrine of rewards under another name.

The Bible is clear that our actions in this life can affect the degree of reward we receive in heaven. Jesus told us to "lay up for yourselves treasures in heaven, where neither moth nor rust consumes and where thieves do not break in and steal. For where your treasure is, there will your heart be also" (Matt. 6:20-21).

Sometimes people imagine that there will be no degrees of reward in heaven—that going to heaven is the only reward that God gives those who believe in him. However, Jesus indicates that individual actions we perform are the subject of rewards.

He warns that certain actions will not receive rewards, such as doing good deeds to receive praise from men (Matt. 6:1-2, 5, 16), while other actions will receive rewards, such as doing good deeds to please God (Matt. 6:4, 6, 18, 10:41-42).

Similarly, St. Paul indicates that some people will enter heaven with greater rewards than others.

He speaks of how individuals build on the foundation of Jesus Christ by doing various things, and he says that one day these works will be tested by fire. Paul then says, "If the work which any man has built on the foundation survives, he will receive a reward. If any man's work is burned up, he will suffer loss, though he himself will be saved, but only as through fire" (1 Cor. 3:14-15).

Some individuals, therefore, will both enter heaven and receive rewards in addition to that, but others will simply enter heaven.

St. Paul also discusses the nature of the rewards that we will receive, writing, "For he [God] will render to every man according to his works: to those who by patience in well-doing seek for glory and honor and immortality, he will give eternal life" (Rom. 2:6-7).

Here he indicates that those who display "patience in well-doing" (literally, "in good work") seek the rewards of "glory and honor and immortality" from God, and this hope does not disappoint, for God gives them "eternal life."

The doctrine of merits has been controversial since the Protestant Reformation, and the claim that eternal life can be merited has been particularly controversial. The concern is that this would mean that we can earn our place before God.

The Church has been firm in rejecting this view. As the *Catechism* puts it: "With regard to God, there is no strict right to any merit on the part of man. Between God and us there is an immeasurable inequality, for we have received everything from him, our Creator" (CCC 2007).

It is in terms of this "strict right" of merit that Pope Benedict XVI wrote, "We cannot—to use the classical expression—'merit' heaven through our works. Heaven is always more than we could merit, just as being loved is never something 'merited,' but always a gift" (*Spe Salvi* 35).

Nevertheless, Scripture does indicate that we will receive rewards, that our actions can lay up "treasures in heaven," and that God will reward patience in good work with glory, honor, immortality, and eternal life. There is a sense, therefore, in which each of these things is understood by the Bible as a reward for what we have done by God's grace.

Good works receive a reward, or become meritorious, not because we earn our place before God but because they are done by God's grace, by God working in our lives, and because he has freely promised to reward them.

"According to the Catholic understanding, good works, made possible by grace and the working of the Holy Spirit, contribute to growth in grace, so that the righteousness that comes from God is preserved and communion with Christ is deepened. When Catholics affirm the 'meritorious' character of good works, they wish to say that, according to the biblical witness, a reward in heaven is promised to these works. Their intention is to emphasize the responsibility of persons for their actions, not to contest the character of those works as gifts, or far less to deny that justification always remains the unmerited gift of grace" (JD 38).

17. What is heaven?

Heaven can be looked at in different ways. One way that the *Catechism* expresses it is: "Heaven is the ultimate end and fulfillment of the deepest human longings, the state of supreme, definitive happiness" (CCC 1024).

However, since God is the ultimate source of human happiness, we cannot experience heaven apart from God. Consequently, heaven can be understood as ultimate spiritual union with God.

And since God shares his love with others, it is a communal experience. "This perfect life with the Most Holy Trinity—this communion of life and love with the Trinity, with the Virgin Mary, the angels, and all the blessed—is called 'heaven'" (CCC 1024). "Heaven is the blessed community of all who are perfectly incorporated into Christ" (CCC 1026).

Scripture uses many images for heaven. The first and most fundamental of these is the sky, which is often referred to as heaven. St. John Paul II explained, "In biblical language 'heaven,' when it is joined to the 'earth,' indicates part of the universe. Scripture says about creation: 'In the beginning God created the heavens and the earth' (Gen. 1:1)" (General Audience, July 21, 1999).

However, the sky came to be used as an image of where God dwells: "Metaphorically speaking, heaven is understood as the dwelling-place of God, who is thus distinguished from human beings (cf. Ps. 104:2-3, 115:16; Isa. 66:1). He sees and judges from the heights of heaven (cf. Ps. 113:4–9) and comes down when he is called upon (cf. Ps. 18:9, 10; 144:5). However the biblical metaphor makes it clear that God does not identify himself with heaven, nor can he be contained in it (cf. 1 Kings 8:27)" (General Audience, July 21, 1999).

Scripture uses other images of heaven as well, though we need to be sensitive to their limitations. The *Catechism* explains, "This mystery of blessed communion with God and all who are in Christ is beyond all understanding and description. Scripture speaks of it in images: life, light, peace, wedding feast, wine of the kingdom, the Father's house, the heavenly Jerusalem, paradise: 'no eye has seen, nor ear heard, nor the heart of man conceived, what God has prepared for those who love him' (1 Cor. 2:9)" (CCC 1027).

We thus shouldn't be overly distracted by modern images of heaven that depict the saints sitting on clouds and playing harps. As St. John Paul II said, "In the context of revelation, we know that the 'heaven' or 'happiness' in which we will find ourselves is neither an abstraction nor a physical place in the clouds, but a living, personal relationship with the Holy Trinity. It is our meeting with the Father which takes place in the risen Christ through the communion of the Holy Spirit" (General Audience, July 21, 1999).

The principal blessing of heaven is union with God, and the Church has a special name for this form of union: "the beatific vision." This is based on passages in Scripture that speak of the faithful being rewarded by being able to see God (Ps. 17:15; Matt. 5:8; 1 Cor. 13:12; 1 John 3:2), though properly speaking God does not have a physical form apart from the Incarnation of Christ and so is invisible.

The *Catechism* explains the beatific vision more fully: "Because of his transcendence, God cannot be seen as he is, unless he himself opens up his mystery to man's immediate contemplation and gives him the capacity for it. The Church calls this contemplation of God in his heavenly glory 'the beatific vision'" (CCC 1028).

Sometimes people imagine that, while experiencing the beatific vision of God, we will not give attention to anything else, but Scripture does not indicate this. In fact, the glimpses of heaven we get in Scripture show the saints and angels expressing concern for events on earth and praying on behalf of others (2 Macc. 15:12-14; Rev. 5:9, 6:9-10, 8:3).

Another misunderstanding, which is even more common today, is that when we die we will remain without our bodies, living as pure spirits. This is not the Christian faith. Although we may be without our bodies for a while, our destiny is to be reunited with them. Just like Jesus, we will be raised from the dead.

St. Paul was emphatic about this: "If the dead are not raised, then Christ has not been raised. If Christ has not been raised, your faith is futile and you are still in your sins" (1 Cor. 15:16-17).

This does not mean that our bodies will be the same as they are now. Paul indicates that they will be changed, comparing our present bodies to seeds that are sown in the ground, only to bring forth something much more glorious: "So is it with the resurrection of the dead. What is sown is perishable, what is raised is imperishable. It is sown in dishonor, it is raised in glory. It is sown in weakness, it is raised in power. It is sown a physical body, it is raised a spiritual body" (1 Cor. 15:42-44).

Heaven thus does not exclude our bodies, and ultimately the saved will live in complete spiritual union with God and others in glorified, bodily form.

18. What is purgatory?

Purgatory is the final purification that God performs for those who died in his friendship but who still need to be purified.

This means that purgatory is not a third destiny, besides heaven and hell. Everyone who goes to purgatory goes to heaven. It's simply a stage of preparing people so that they have the purity needed to experience heaven.

Neither is purgatory a "second chance" after death. "It is appointed for men to die once, and after that comes judgment" (Heb. 9:27). There are no second chances. You either die in God's friendship, or you don't.

Sometimes people ask why, if Christ died for our sins, we should experience purgatory. The answer is found in the fact that, even after we come to God and are forgiven and justified, we still struggle with sin and its consequences. It may be God's will that the eternal consequences of our sins be forgiven, but Christian experience shows that we are not made perfect all in a flash.

During the Christian life, we continue to struggle with sin and, by God's grace, to grow in holiness. It's also God's will that we bear some of the consequences of our sins, which is one of the reasons that we fast and do other forms of penance.

Many people die in God's friendship rather than in mortal sin, but few of us have been fully freed from sin and its consequences. As a result, we need to be purified before we enter heaven—for Scripture tells us that "nothing unclean shall enter it" (Rev. 21:27). Heaven is being fully united with God, and since he is infinitely holy, nothing that is still impure can be fully united with him. Consequently, Scripture exhorts us to seek "the holiness without which no one will see the Lord" (Heb. 12:14).

The process of growing in holiness is sometimes called "sanctification," and thus one can think of purgatory as simply the final stage of sanctification, where we are fully freed and liberated from sin.

If nothing impure enters heaven then, between death and heaven, there must be a purification.

We do not know a great deal about how God chooses to accomplish this purification. St. Paul uses the image of fire—a frequent biblical image for purification and transformation—when he speaks of people who have built imperfectly on the foundation of Christ. He describes their works being tested by fire, and he says that "If any man's work is burned up, he will suffer loss, though he himself will be saved, but only as through fire" (1 Cor. 3:15). He thus compares the experience to escaping through flames.

Pope Benedict XVI noted that "Some recent theologians are of the opinion that the fire which both burns and saves is Christ himself, the Judge and Savior. The encounter with him is the decisive act of judgment. Before his gaze all falsehood melts away. This encounter with him, as it burns us, transforms and frees us, allowing us to become truly ourselves. All that we build during our lives can prove to be mere straw, pure bluster, and it collapses. Yet in the pain of this encounter, when the impurity and sickness of our lives become evident to us, there lies salvation. His gaze, the touch of his heart heals us through an undeniably painful transformation 'as through fire.' But it is a blessed pain, in which the holy power of his love sears through us like a flame, enabling us to become totally ourselves and thus totally of God" (*Spe Salvi* 47).

We also do not know how long this process takes. Jesus told the good thief, "today you will be with me in Paradise" (Luke 23:43), and Scripture speaks of those who are alive on the last day being transformed "in the twinkling of an eye" (1 Cor. 15:52).

Pope Benedict stated: "It is clear that we cannot calculate the 'duration' of this transforming burning in terms of the chronological measurements of this world. The transforming 'moment' of this encounter eludes earthly time-reckoning—it is the heart's time" (*Spe Salvi* 47).

It is clear, though, that we can help those who experience this purification, just as we can pray for those who are growing in holiness here on earth. Regardless of precisely when and how the final purification occurs, God can apply our prayers to those experiencing it.

Thus, the practice of praying for the dead was used by the Jewish people even before the time of Christ (2 Macc. 12:38-45), and it has been part of Christian practice from the very beginning (see Jimmy Akin, *The Fathers Know Best*, ch. 57).

19. What is hell?

The New Testament makes it clear that God "desires all men to be saved and to come to the knowledge of the truth" (1 Tim. 2:4), but it also indicates that we can reject God's offer of salvation.

"To die in mortal sin without repenting and accepting God's merciful love means remaining separated from him for ever by our own free choice. This state of definitive self-exclusion from communion with God and the blessed is called 'hell'" (CCC 1033).

Pope Benedict XVI explained, "There can be people who have totally destroyed their desire for truth and readiness to love, people for whom everything has become a lie, people who have lived for hatred and have suppressed all love within themselves. This is a terrifying thought, but alarming profiles of this type can be seen in certain figures of our own history. In such people all would be beyond remedy and the destruction of good would be irrevocable: this is what we mean by the word *hell*" (*Spe Salvi* 45).

In describing hell, the New Testament uses images such as fire (Matt. 13:50; Mark 9:43; Rev. 14:10, 21:8) and being excluded from the presence of God (Matt. 8:12, 22:13, 25:30; 2 Thess. 1:9).

The images that Scripture uses for hell are meant to give us a way of envisioning what takes place in the next life, but because we do not have access to it, we must recognize the limits of these images.

St. John Paul II stated, "The images of hell that Sacred Scripture presents to us must be correctly interpreted. They show the complete frustration and emptiness of life without God. Rather than a place, hell indicates the state of those who freely and definitively separate themselves from God, the source of all life and joy" (General Audience, July 28, 1999).

We, therefore, must leave the details of precisely how hell works—where and how the suffering takes place—to God. What is important for us is to recognize the seriousness of the situation and the need to make sure that we are united with God, who is our ultimate source of happiness.

"Hell's principal punishment consists of eternal separation from God in whom alone man can have the life and happiness for which he was created and for which he longs" (CCC 1057).

Although Scripture and the Church use the language of punishment in connection with hell, this has to be properly understood. "It is not a punishment imposed externally by God but a development of premises already set by people in this life . . . 'Eternal damnation,' therefore, is not attributed to God's initiative because in his merciful love he can only desire the salvation of the beings he created. In reality, it is the creature who closes himself to his love. Damnation consists precisely in definitive separation from God, freely chosen by the human person and confirmed with death that seals his choice forever. God's judgment ratifies this state" (St. John Paul II, General Audience, July 28, 1999).

Consequently, contrary to the claims of some, "God predestines no one to go to hell; for this, a willful turning away from God (a mortal sin) is necessary, and persistence in it until the end" (CCC 1037).

It is thus not so much that God chooses to send a person to hell. Rather, the person chooses to remain separate from God, to reject his offer of love and forgiveness, and God respects the person's choice.

At the end of life, our choice becomes definitive. We will not change our mind after death, which is why both heaven and hell last forever (cf. CCC 1035).

But as long as we are still alive, we can choose to turn to God, no matter what we have done, no matter how bad our sins have been.

"There is no offense, however serious, that the Church cannot forgive. There is no one, however wicked and guilty, who may not confidently hope for forgiveness, provided his repentance is honest. Christ who died for all men desires that in his Church the gates of forgiveness should always be open to anyone who turns away from sin" (CCC 982).

Consequently, "The thought of hell—and even less the improper use of biblical images—must not create anxiety or despair, but is a necessary and healthy reminder of freedom" (St. John Paul II, General Audience, July 28, 1999).

"The Church prays that no one should be lost: 'Lord, let me never be parted from you.' If it is true that no one can save himself, it is also true that God 'desires all men to be saved' (1 Tim. 2:4), and that for him 'all things are possible' (Matt. 19:26)" (CCC 1058).

20. Is there salvation outside the Church?

The Church Fathers are famous for the saying, "Outside the Church, no salvation." This is one way of expressing the necessity of the Christian religion—and Christ's Church—for salvation.

It's a theme that goes all the way back to Jesus when he told his disciples, "I am the way, and the truth, and the life; no one comes to the Father, but by me" (John 14:6).

The early Christians understood this, and St. Peter boldly told the authorities of his day that "there is salvation in no one else, for there is no other name under heaven given among men by which we must be saved" (Acts 4:12).

For a person to know that Jesus is God's Christ, the Savior of mankind, and to refuse to repent, believe, and be baptized into his Church would be to reject salvation on the terms that God offers it, and thus to reject salvation itself. That is why the Church Fathers said that there is no salvation outside the Church.

The early Christians also recognized that many people aren't in that situation. They may not have joined the Church, but it may not have been through their own fault. In those cases, they didn't knowingly and deliberately reject God's offer of salvation.

So what about people in this situation?

In the ancient world, and even today, many had no chance to respond to the Christian message because they never heard it. Thus, when St. Paul talked to the people of Athens, he told them God "overlooked" the times of idolatry in the hopes that men would "feel after him and find him." He even indicated that some of their own thinkers had arrived at a partial knowledge of God (Acts 17:22-31).

In his letter to the Romans, Paul speaks of how some Gentiles, who have never heard the word of God, nevertheless obey God's law, because it is written on their hearts. He then seems to hold out the possibility of salvation for them, saying that their consciences may excuse them on the day of judgment (Rom. 2:14-16).

This theme was also picked up by the Church Fathers. St. Justin Martyr held that those who had not heard the gospel could be saved if they lived "according to reason," and the Greek word he used for "reason" is *logos*—the same word that St. John used to refer to the preincarnate Christ in the prologue of his Gospel (John 1:1-18).

The idea was that, without explicitly hearing Christ preached, some Gentiles lived according to reason, according to the Logos, and thus had an implicit connection with Christ that would enable them to be saved. It was still through Christ that they would be saved, though they did not know that in this life.

Therefore, today the Church recognizes the necessity of Jesus and his Church for salvation, but it also recognizes that some people who are not fully incorporated into his Church can still be related to it in a way that makes salvation possible for them.

Thus the *Catechism* states, "The Church, a pilgrim now on earth, is necessary for salvation: The one Christ is the mediator and the way of salvation; he is present to us in his body which is the Church. He himself explicitly asserted the necessity of faith and baptism, and thereby affirmed at the same time the necessity of the

Church which men enter through baptism as through a door. Hence they could not be saved who, knowing that the Catholic Church was founded as necessary by God through Christ, would refuse either to enter it or to remain in it" (CCC 846).

It goes on to state, "This affirmation is not aimed at those who, through no fault of their own, do not know Christ and his Church: Those who, through no fault of their own, do not know the Gospel of Christ or his Church, but who nevertheless seek God with a sincere heart, and, moved by grace, try in their actions to do his will as they know it through the dictates of their conscience—those too may achieve eternal salvation" (CCC 847).

The fact that it's possible for people to be saved without being fully incorporated into the Church doesn't mean that they don't need to hear the message of Christ or that we don't need to evangelize them. The more light and grace they have, the better!

"Although in ways known to himself God can lead those who, through no fault of their own, are ignorant of the Gospel, to that faith without which it is impossible to please him, the Church still has the obligation and also the sacred right to evangelize all men" (CCC 848).

Jesus himself said: "Go therefore and make disciples of all nations, baptizing them in the name of the Father and of the Son and of the Holy Spirit" (Matt. 28:19).

About the Author

Jimmy Akin is an internationally known author and speaker. As the senior apologist at Catholic Answers, he has more than twenty years' experience defending and explaining the Faith.

A convert from Protestantism, Jimmy has an extensive background in the Bible, theology, the Church Fathers, philosophy, canon law, and liturgy.

He is the author of hundreds of articles and dozens of publications, including the best-selling books *The Fathers Know Best* and *The Drama of Salvation*.

Jimmy is a weekly guest on the national radio program *Catholic Answers Live*, a regular contributor to *Catholic Answers Magazine*, and a popular blogger and podcaster. His personal website is JimmyAkin.com.

Become part of the team.
Help support Catholic Answers.

Catholic Answers is an apostolate dedicated to serving Christ by bringing the fullness of Catholic truth to the world. We help good Catholics become better Catholics, bring former Catholics "home," and lead non-Catholics into the fullness of the Faith.

Catholic Answers neither asks for nor receives financial support from any diocese. The majority of its annual income is in the form of donations from individual supporters like you.

To make a donation by phone using your credit card, please speak with one of our customer service representatives at 888-291-8000.

To make a donation by check, please send a check payable to "Catholic Answers" to:

> Catholic Answers
> 2020 Gillespie Way
> El Cajon, CA 92020

To make a donation online, visit **catholic.com**.

Catholic Answers
TO EXPLAIN & DEFEND THE FAITH

catholic.com